1

Published and bound in the United States of America, 2017.

Book Cover photograph made from statue of the Archangel Michael standing on the head of the evil angel, Lucifer. Cover Photograph © W. Mike Howell, 2017.

ISBN: 978-0-692-95923-7

ANGELS: GOOD AND EVIL

a collection of original free-verse poems

by

W. Mike Howell

CONTENTS

DEDICATION

This book is dedicated to the love of my life, Mary Kirkland Howell, who has stood by my side during our six decades of life together. She has selfishly abandoned many of her own dreams in order to encourage me in mine.

FOREWORD

Dr. Mike Howell is a renowned professor and scholar in the biological sciences. He has published over fifty peer-reviewed scientific papers in cytogenetics, chromosome structure, vertebrate taxonomy and evolutionary processes. He possesses authoritative knowledge of the theories and evidence of evolution and of other sciences of the natural world, origins and growths and functions. He knows professionally, then, all the natural conditions that for many undergird an atheistic conviction. This, however, is not Mike's conviction. Scholarly texts may serve as his books for the living, but the Bible is his book of life.

This present book about angels is not a cold classification of biblical references to angels; it flows from the heart and soul of a spiritually warm and compassionate faith, a man with a Christ-centered heart, who knows that the language of life must be felt, like song and poetry, must find in God the whole truth, beyond and earth-living, the truth like that within the

Bible and in the life of Christ. The Christian Bible, the Holy Bible, believes in angels for our sake, and reveals for us the power and mission, the place of angels in the whole truth of God's purpose and providence.

Mike has "seen" deeply into angelic life with a scholar's diligence, a disciple's dedication, a poet's voice. This is free verse, poetic prose; nothing rhymes by scheme, the cadence is not a sing song, but the language that reaches up with emotion ready to burst into heavenly elation and praise.

What can we learn about angels? How can we meet them? I can conclude from this book that angels are perhaps distinct emanations from God---a reaching out, a lifting up, a transforming, with a central message that all of us often need: "Do not be afraid."

The book lifts the veil on angels:

The recognition of angels, eleven characteristics,,

The holy mission of angels.

The role of angels in spiritual salvation and eternal hope,

The book recognizes too the first Hell's Angel, Satan, the nature of Satan, his strategies and goal, our defenses and the consequences of our yielding to Satan, Satan's catastrophic effect upon the march of time.

What we can learn about angels, as we become open to them, opens the Bible anew, confirming for us perhaps more deeply the indisputable truths about God, Christ the Savior, the holy spirit and God's emanations-- His angels--visiting earth. A quote from Mike's book: "Angels are ideas that flow from the mind of God altering the course of human history... ."

From this book we can understand the mission of angels and acquire something beyond merely biblical knowledge: if we can come to know and to believe in angels, we may acquire a new dimension of faith that can lift our daily lives and give us a holy vision to live by.

The mission of angels, made apparent in this book, is to prepare us for and lead us into a future that is ours, appointed within God's will distinctively for us.

Charles T. Workman, Ph.D.
Professor *emeritus,* Department of English
Samford University

INTRODUCTION

As a scientist, I was at first reluctant to write about angels. But, they are, after all, creations of God. And, as a Christian, I felt compelled to learn the scriptural truth about these spiritual beings as recorded in the Holy Bible. That sacred book was the source of my information about angels, and my poetic interpretations of those scriptures.

All of the poems were written in free-style (no rules of poetry apply). They are all original and informational. Some may not seem like poetry, but just a story. But, to me, the poetry seemed to flow onto the pages from a light within my mind.

I have included poems about both good and evil angels. It is true, Satan (Lucifer) is an angel, ruler of evil here on earth. He was cast down to earth from Heaven when he and his demonic angels tried to overthrow God. So, Satan was included, often as the main character in some of the poems. *It is important to emphasize that God's heavenly angels are not to be worshipped.* They are only God's messengers. Jesus Christ (God Himself) is the only one to be worshipped by Christians. And, earthly angels, Satan (Lucifer or Devil) and his satanic demonic angels, are to be avoided at all costs. They have left trails of destruction throughout the world and their goal is to overcome God and all things that are good and righteous. I hope that these poems accurately reflect biblical truths.

---W. Mike Howell, 2017

ACKNOWLEDGMENTS

I express my sincere thanks to those who have helped and encouraged me throughout the writing of this book. Words cannot express my deep appreciation to Dr. Charles T. Workman , English professor *emeritus,* who spent untold hours reading, editing, and helping me with the process of book publishing. Glenn Waddell, President of the Birmingham Theological Seminary, critically read the manuscript for possible biblical inconsistencies. Scott Linton, Lawyer and an expert on the poet Milton, carefully read and made constructive comments. My wife, Mary Howell, read and suggested valuable comments on each poem, and agonized with me as I trudged through Photoshop while preparing the manuscript for publication. My sister, Diane Howell Coffey, gave me continuous support throughout the writing of this book. Claude Wegscheider helped me in untold ways during the past few years. Without these individuals, this book would never have been written.

ANGELS: GOOD AND EVIL - THE BIBLICAL FACTS

Too many people
Have too many angel stories.
Exaggerations abound.
Misconceptions all around.
"Angelmania,"
a modern term invented,
to describe
the miraculous
acts supposedly performed
by these supernatural beings.
Not all of mania tales can be true.
So,
Where can we go to find the real truth
about angels?
Practical minded people would seek
the actual source of angels'
origins, powers and actions--the Holy Bible.
That is where the stories of angels are documented,
and where they perform their Godly duties.
God had a purpose in creating them--
They are His messengers.
They are sent by God to carry out
His varied wishes.
Angels display their actions only as God commands
them.
They can be compassionate comforters
to people who are hurting.
They can be powerful and destructive to those

who are spiritually corrupt
and disobedient to God.
Evil angels (Satan and his demons) oppose God,
his Son, Jesus Christ,
and the Holy Spirit.
Angels are mentioned throughout
the Bible,
in thirty-four books,
from Genesis to Revelation.
Some scholars say the word angel is
mentioned over one-hundred and three times
in the Old Testament,
Ninety-three in the New Testament.
But other scholars argue that
these may not always be angels
but theophanies---manifestations of God.
But, when did God create them?
No one knows,
The Holy Bible does not say.
But, in the book of Job,
God says that the "sons of God"
were with Him when he laid
the foundations of the earth,
and they all shouted for joy (Job 38:7).
Many biblical scholars claim
that the "sons of God"
referred to His angels.
So, angels were already created
before the earth's creation.
Theologians argue that there are
several kinds or levels of angels:

16

Cherubim, Seraphim, Archangels, Dominions,
Powers and Principalities.
Most, however, recognize Cherubim,
Seraphim, and Archangels.
Satan (Lucifer) is also an angel,
a rogue, vilely evil angel,
who stands apart from the good angels.
Accompanying him is his massive
army of demonic, evil angels.
In our scientific world of today,
it seems ludicrous that such
unseen entities as angels should exist.
But, the Bible is crystal clear and dead serious
about the existence and role of angels.
At least two kinds of angels
were present in the book of Genesis:
Holy angels (the Cherubim),
and evil angels (Satan and his demons).
Angels do not always have a human-like form
but, as spirits, they can easily morph
into a variety of forms.
The first angel to appear in Genesis
was Satan,
An evil angel who has perpetually fought savagely
and cunningly against
God and his goodness.
In Genesis 3:1,
Satan took on the form of a serpent:
"Now the serpent was more cunning
than any beast of the field
which the Lord God had made... ."

After the serpent had deceived Eve
to eat of the forbidden fruit
from the tree of knowledge,
God banished Eve and Adam
from the garden.
Genesis 3:24 states,
"So He drove out the man; and He placed
cherubim at the east of the garden of Eden,
and a flaming sword which turned every way,
to guard the way to the tree of life."
Theologians do not fully understand
the origin of the term "cherubim,"
but it is a kind of angel.
As stated above, theologians usually recognize
at least three different kinds
of angels: cherubim, seraphim, and archangels.
Each kind has different roles and characteristics.
It is debated whether "powers" and "principalities"
are also ranks among the holy angels.
In truth, Satan is not a holy angel,
but an evil angel,
He is enemy number one to God.
We must get to know Satan
as the most corruptive force
in the lives of all humanity.
We cannot ignore him
as his deceptive nature
will suck us into his powerful vortex
of greed and evil.
He is referred to by
various names in the Bible--

more names than the list given here:
Satan, Lucifer, Devil, Antichrist,
Angel of the Bottomless Pit, Baal,
Beast, Beelzebub, Chief of Demons, Evil One,
Leviathan, Ruler of the Darkness, Serpent,
Tempter and 666.

The intellectual and liberal Sadducees
did not believe in angels.
But, Jesus rebuked them saying, (Matt. 22:29-30)
"You are mistaken,
not knowing the scriptures
nor the power of God."
"For in the resurrection they neither
marry nor are given in marriage,
but are like angels of God in heaven."
So, Angels do not marry,
do not have children,
do not die,
and were all created by God
at the creation.
Therefore, reason would have us believe
that the number of angels today
is the same number as always.
How many angels are there?
The Bible doesn't give a definitive number,
but alludes to an extraordinary high number.
Revelation 5:11 states, "Then I looked, and I
heard the voice of many angels around the throne,
the living creatures, and the elders;
and the number of them

was ten thousand times ten thousand,
and, thousands of thousands."
In Luke 20:34-36, Jesus tells us
that worthy people,
resurrected from the dead,
are equal to the angels,
in that they do not marry
nor are given in marriage,
nor can they die anymore.
Being like the angels,
means that the resurrected person,
with an immaterial spirit,
will not age as normal humans do.
Though the resurrected will become a spirit,
they will still be able to move,
touch, and miraculously affect
the physical world around them (Matt. 28:2;
Acts 12:7; 2 Chronicles 32:21; Genesis 19:11;
2 Kings 19:35).
Resurrected people will be knowledgeable,
but will not know all things
as God does.
Angels are emotional beings as evidenced
in Luke 15:10, which states,
"Likewise, I say to you, there is joy
in the presence of angels of God
over one sinner who repents."

The characteristics of Satan and his
demonic angels must be also recognized.
First, the evil angels have many of the

20

same characteristics of good angels:
immaterial spirits, ability to change form,
emotions, ageless, sexless, and so forth.
They differ, however, in being weaker
in strength and intellectual prowess
than the good angels.
In a war in Heaven, the evil angels
were beaten by the Archangel Michael
who commanded God's army
of holy angels (Rev. 12:7-9).
The Satanic angels are depraved, conniving,
evil, perverse, unclean,
murdering, and lying spirits (Mark 1:23; John 8:44).
These unclean spirits
now recognize their wretched,
ugly, and miserable existence.
This must be shocking, even to them,
after once enjoying the glorious blessings
of God in Heaven.
What a blundering, eternal mistake they all made
by following Satan, the Chief of Demons!
Instead of belonging to a Kingdom of Light,
they now are charter members of
the Kingdom of Darkness (2 Peter 2:4)
led by the Prince of Darkness.
Satan, himself, is cocky, pushy, and self-assertive.
Imagine this brash evil spirit tempting
the Son of God in the wilderness (Matt. 4:1-11).
Satan and his evil angels deviously planned
the crucifixion of Jesus.
In doing so,

They plotted their own self-destruction.
They will be bound with chains,
cast into hell and condemned
to eternal fire (Matt. 25:41; Jude 1:6; 2 Peter 2-4).
For those evil spirits,
there will be no second chance for repentance
and salvation.
Never again will they experience the
blissful, holy state they once enjoyed in Heaven.
The story of the angels
is also the story of mankind.
Obedience to Jesus Christ
credited to us by the grace of God (Eph. 2:8-9),
will insure our place in Heaven.
Conversely, obedience to Satan
will preserve our place in
a Kingdom of Darkness,
bound for eternity in chains,
with no chance of escape
from the agonizing pain,
and the stench of burning flesh.
But, even this does not exceed
the unending torture suffered by
the eternal absence
from the Light of God.

(References: Scripture passages in text above taken from Holy Bible, The New King James Version, 1984 ed., Thomas Nelson Publishers)

WAR IN HEAVEN

Biblical scholars,
as usual, do not agree
on certain parts of the Holy Bible,
and especially the final book
in the New Testament.
Some argue that no one knows
who wrote the book of The Revelation.
Most Christians erroneously call
this book, "Revelations,"
a pluralizing misconception.
But, if we look carefully,
the official title of this book is
"The Revelation of Jesus Christ."
Most present day scholars and non-scholars
believe the author to be
John, the Apostle.
Revelation 1:1-2 states,
"The Revelation of Jesus Christ,
which God gave Him to show
His servants--things which must
shortly take place.
And He sent and signified it by
His angel to His servant John,
who bore witness to the word of God,
and to the testimony
of Jesus Christ,
and to all things that he saw."
Revelation 12: 7-9 states,
"And war broke out in heaven:

Michael and his angels fought
against the dragon; and the
dragon and his angels fought,
but they did not prevail,
nor was a place found for them
in heaven any longer.
So the great dragon of old,
called the Devil and Satan,
who deceives the whole world;
he was cast to earth,
and his angels
were cast out with him."
This is good news, and bad news.
Good news that Satan and his demonic pals
were kicked out of Heaven.
Bad news that he and his evil angels
have been unleashed
upon all of humanity.
We must continuously be alert
and vigilant,
as none of us are
immune to the powerful deceptive powers
of these evil ones.

(References In Text Above: Holy Bible, New King James Version,
Thomas Nelson Publishers)

MESSIANIC MESSENGERS

I believe that
God leads me in many ways.
Oftentimes I do not know that
He is conveying information
to me...
information that helps
me maintain my Christian composure.
During times of intense anger
and misunderstandings with others,
I often find myself strangely
reversing my desire for vengeance
and retaliation.
Instead of responding to others disrespectfully,
I find myself responding humbly
and in a Godly manner.
This reversal in my intended actions
could have been a
message directly from God,
nudging me,
as a believer,
into choosing the righteous,
forgiving response.
Or, He could have sent an angel--
A messianic messenger--
to guide me
in making the right choices
in moments of moral decisions.
Psalm 91:11 states,
"For He shall give His angels

charge over you, to keep you
in all His ways."

(Reference: Holy Bible. The New King James Version.1984 ed.,
Thomas Nelson Publishers: Psalm 91:11.)

SATAN'S BEAUTY

How can human society
get religious things so wrong?
Ask a child to draw a picture
of Satan.
The drawing will likely depict
a horrible looking,
demon-like creature,
part human, part animal,
with fang like teeth, pointed ears,
a long tail
and holding a pitch fork...
and all will be colored in red.
Biblical scriptures describe
Satan very differently.
Isaiah 14:12 calls Satan "Lucifer,"
a name that means "light,"
or "shining star."
In Ezekiel 28:12-15
God described Satan
as a beautiful angel,
a very wise one.
He was covered with every
precious stone known,
including diamonds, sapphires,
emeralds and gold.
In Ezekiel 28:15,
God stated,
"You were perfect in your ways
from the day you were created,

Till iniquity was found in you."
Lucifer was so prideful
in his wisdom and beauty,
that he set out to dethrone God
and become a ruler-god himself.
He gathered around himself
one-third of all the heavenly angels
in a rebellion against God.
However, his angelic forces
were overwhelmed
by the Archangel Michael
and his good angels.
Lucifer and his evil angels (demons)
were banished from Heaven
down to earth.
But Satan was not through
in trying to defeat God.
His goal, and that of these demon angels,
is to turn every earthly person
against the one true God.
Even though he was banished from Heaven
He was not banished from earth.
Satan and his demonic angels
are still in control of evil
in our world.
They have blinded the minds
of those who do not believe
in the light of
Jesus Christ.
At times,
it seems to the modern Christian

that Satan and his evil crew
have gained control
in our world.
However, in the end,
when Jesus
appears in all His glory,
Satan and his demonic troops
will forever be conquered.
1 Corinthians 15:24-26 states,
"Then comes the end,
when He delivers the
kingdom of God the Father,
when He puts an end
to all rule and all
authority and power.
For He must reign till He has
put all enemies under His feet.
The last enemy that will be
destroyed is death."
Revelation 20:1-3 reveals
Satan's horrible fate quite clearly.
"Then I saw an angel coming
down from heaven,
having the key
to the bottomless pit
and a great chain in his hand.
He laid hold of the dragon,
that serpent of old,
who is the Devil and Satan,
and bound him for a thousand years;
and he cast him into the bottomless pit,

and shut him up,
and set a seal on him,
so that he should deceive the nations
no more
till the thousand years were finished.
But after these things
he must be released for
a little while."
So Lucifer (Satan) had
everything one would
need or want while he was
a heavenly angel.
But Satan desired
not only to be like God,
but to become
God himself.
One might wonder how
Heaven will one day look
to the defeated Satan...
as he looks skyward...
from the bottomless pit
while being
helplessly bound
by unbreakable chains?

(References: Holy Bible: Isaiah 14:12; Ezekiel 28:12-15;
1 Corinthians 15:24-26; Revelation 20:1-3.
The New King James Version.1984 ed.,
Thomas Nelson Publishers).

THE GREAT MASQUERADER

The Old Testament
Describes how
the angel Lucifer (or Satan),
deceived one-third of the
heavenly angels,
into following him
and his evil plan
to overthrow
God and his heavenly Kingdom.
Lucifer had his eyes set
on owning that throne.
So a war broke out in Heaven
between Lucifer's angels,
and the archangel Michael and
his army of good angels.
Michael's angels triumphed and
Lucifer and his evil angels
were cast out of Heaven and
down to Earth.
The Scriptures then declared
"Therefore rejoice, O heavens,
and you who dwell in them!
Woe to the inhabitants of the earth
And the sea!
For the devil has come down to you,
having great wrath...".
Today Satan and his followers
are clever deceivers.
They can masquerade as

humans, animals or objects,
trying to persuade all peoples
of the earth to become
disciples of his satanic kingdom.
Lucifer (now called Satan)
may be likened to those
who attend a Masquerade Ball,
One never knows who is behind the mask.
Satan always wears a mask,
Maybe pretending to be your best friend,
Or whispering in your ear
about the extraordinary pleasures
you would gain
if you would only partake of
drugs, sexual encounters,
or break God's commandments.
Fortunately, for true believers,
Christ has given us the power
to rip away Satan's mask and
reveal him as he is...and tell
Him face-to-face, as Jesus did
When He proclaimed,
"Away with you Satan!
For it is written,
You shall serve the Lord your God,
and Him only you shall serve."
Some Christians think that,
as believers,
we do not
have the power to direct Satan
to do anything.

But, the Archangel Michael,
in contending with the devil,
dared not bring against him a
reviling accusation,
but said, "The Lord rebuke you!"
Satan cannot exist in the presence
of the words of God.
When Satan tempts you,
cite the words of Jesus and Jude above,
and you can almost feel
the hot whirlwinds
of Satan as he flees from these holy
words that pierce his body
and agonize his evil soul.

(References: Holy Bible: Revelations 12:7-12;
12:12; Matthew 4:10 Revelations 12:7-12; Matthew 4:10,
Jude 9; New King James Version. 1984 ed.,
Thomas Nelson Publishers).

THE MISUNDERSTOOD ANGELS

The wise old man scratched his head
and wondered,
"How can a Christian believe in God
and not in angels?"
With this thought,
he quietly drifted off to sleep and
dreamed that he was on a busy
city sidewalk asking
any person he met,
"Are you a Christian?"
Many said,
"Yes, I am."
Then, the aged man asked them,
"Do you believe in God?"
All invariably said,
"Yes I do."
The man then asked,
"Do you believe in Angels?"
A long pause ensued...
followed by a sheepish reply,
"Well, I'm not so sure about angels."
The old man then pondered,
"Why do Christians believe that God created
all things,
but do not believe in angels?"
Then, the aged and wrinkled man
thought, "Goodness, the name angel,
appears in the Bible over
one-hundred times.

God used angels in innumerable
and important ways.
Does the average person ever really
read the Holy Scriptures? "
The Bible clearly states
in Psalm 148:2-5,
"Praise Him all his angels;
Praise Him, all His hosts!
Praise Him, sun and moon;
Praise Him, all you stars of light!
Praise Him, you heavens of heavens,
and the waters above the heavens!
Let them praise the name of the Lord,
For He commanded and they were created."
After these thoughts and a mumbled
prayer for the non-believers
the old man, once again, drifted into a deep
and peaceful sleep.

(Reference: Holy Bible: Psalm 148:2-5. New King James Version,
1984 ed., Thomas Nelson Publishers)

THE ORIGIN OF ISRAEL

Jealousy, deceit, thievery,
cunning, a stolen birthright,
a planned murder
and fleeing from a certain death--
these are events that happen between
flesh and blood relatives--
things that happen even between
twins.
Such twins were Esau and Jacob,
born to parents Isaac and Rebekah,
and grandsons of Abraham.
Not identical twins
as one first imagines,
but fraternal twins.
Each genetically distinct,
and behaviorally
as different as sibling brothers born
years apart.
Esau was strong, hairy,
an outdoorsman, a hunter...
a man's man,
the favorite son of Isaac.
Jacob, a fair young boy,
with smooth, non-hairy arms,
who liked to stay near the tents--
a mother's boy.
Rebekah doted on Jacob,
showering favoritism on him
in many ways--some good,

some evil.
All was good with this family
until violence erupted,
like a stroke of blinding lightning
from a vicious thunderstorm.
But this violence was triggered by
a stolen birthright...
a theft that shattered this family into
broken human fragments.
Amazingly,
out of the
family turbulence and hatred that ensued,
arose the nation of Israel,
and its twelve tribes!
The story is a simple human story.
But it does not end like human stories.
The story terminates with the birth
of the nation of Israel.
The story goes much like this.
Esau, the first born twin,
was the rightful owner of
his birthright.
He had legitimate claim
to receive Isaac's blessings.
But Rebekah wanted that birthright
for Jacob.
Rebekah and Jacob tricked the aging Isaac,
whose eyesight was failing,
by making Jacob's arm feel hairy to Isaac,
using lamb's wool as an arm covering.
Isaac fell for the evil trickery

and gave Jacob the blessing that belonged
to Esau.
Esau was furious.
Esau must have felt horribly dejected--
his mother connived the evil plan,
while his treacherous brother carried it out.
He vowed that he would kill Jacob
as soon as their father died.
Rebekah found out about
Esau's murderous plan
to kill Jacob,
so she warned Jacob to leave immediately.
Jacob was to go to Padam Aram
to the house of Laban,
Rebekah's brother.
So Jacob fled his homeland.
After a long anxious journey,
Jacob was tired and sleepy.
He laid down on the ground
and placed a large stone
beneath his head
for a pillow.
Jacob then fell into a deep sleep.
In a vivid dream,
Jacob saw a long stairway
that extended from Heaven
all the way down to Earth.
And, on the stairway,
he saw *angels* descending
and ascending.
"And behold, the LORD stood

above it and said: "I am the LORD
God of Abraham your father and
the God of Isaac; the land on which
you lie I will give to you
and your descendants."
(Genesis 28:13).
Jacob felt that the spot where he had lain
his head was the "Gate to Heaven" itself.
He poured oil on the stone
and named the place "Bethel."
meaning the "House of God."
After several years of living
with his uncle Laban
and marrying two of his daughters,
Jacob tired of Laban's devious treatment of him,
so he fled with his two wives and eleven sons.
With Laban chasing him from behind,
and Esau, ahead of him, vowing to kill him,
Jacob was caught in the middle of a
dilemma.
He sent his two wives and children
across the river to lessen Esau's rage
by presenting him with gifts.
But, Jacob stayed behind.
He was exhausted from fleeing.
That night he fell into a deep sleep.
And, a Man (some scholars say an "angel,"
others say "God"; we will use "angel.")
wrestled with Jacob until the breaking of day
at which time the angelic being
hit Jacob in the hip,

injuring it to the extent that he never
again walked without a limp.
This blow ended the fight,
Jacob then asked the angel to bless him.
So the angel asked, "Tell me your name, I pray."
And He said, "Jacob."
And he said, "Your name shall no longer
be called Jacob, but Israel; for you have
struggled with God and with men,
and have prevailed."
When Jacob (Israel) met face-to-face with Esau,
his brother unexpectedly embraced him
and the two made peace.
Jacob lived a long, God-fearing life from
that point onward.
He had twelve sons,
each of whom was declared head
of one of the twelve tribes
of the nation called "Israel."
He became one of the most revered patriarchs
in the Bible,
and established the land of Israel
that God had promised
his grandfather, Abraham,
many years before.
So, Jacob had at times been a schemer,
deceiver, liar, manipulator and thief.
He struggled with God most of
his life.
But as he needed God more and more,
his faith grew.

It reached its culmination during Jacob's
wrestling with the angel
throughout the night.
When the angel injured Jacob's hip,
Jacob became a new man,
a repentant one,
and, with a new name, "Israel."
Jacob had finally given complete
control of his life to God.
One moral of Jacob's story is that
while we may be as imperfect
as the young Jacob,
God can take our imperfections
and spiritual brokenness,
and put us back together again,
He can heal our sin-torn soul.

(References: Holy Bible: Text based on Genesis chapters 27-36;
Genesis 28:13. New King James Version. 1984 ed.,
Thomas Nelson Publishers)

WHERE SPIRITS DWELL

Other worlds,
other dimensions.
Dwelling places of
both good and evil spirits.
Hell for Satan and his legions
of demonic angels,
Heaven for the Trinity...
God, Jesus Christ, Holy Spirit.
And home of God's
Holy Angels.
No human has ever been there
and returned to tell
of either place.
But some have had visions
of these two spiritual realms.
Hell is, or will be, burning with fire,
filled with smells of
burning flesh,
with unending screams
of those who were
earthly sinners and
evil persons...a horrible
dwelling place for one's eternal spirit.
The antithesis of Hell is Heaven.
It is incomprehensible.
The limited mind of man
is incapable of even imagining
what it is like...
a place of untold beauty,

ethereal music,
with all spiritual beings
singing praises
and worshipping God.
Only Jesus Christ, Satan and angels
have knowledge of both
Heaven and Earth.
They have been to both worlds.
Earth is now the semi-permanent home
of Satan.
Hell will be his future
and permanent dwelling place.
Heaven is the home of Jesus Christ.
Earth will eventually be Jesus'
temporary dwelling place
for a thousand years.
Then He will return to Heaven.
To give credence that
Heaven is a real place,
God himself, in the form of Jesus,
came from this
Holy dwelling to tell
His highest creation, mankind,
that Heaven is real...
but accessible only
to a select few.
And how, after death, one's spirit
can enter that godly realm,
but only if he/she repents
of all sins
and believes in His Word.

Before Jesus' death,
He told his disciples,
"In my Father's house are
Many mansions;
If it were not so,
I would have told you.
I go to prepare a place for you.
And if I go and prepare a
place for you,
I will come again and receive you
to Myself;
that where I am,
there you may be also."
(Holy Bible: John 14:2,3)
There are two choices,
but only one spiritual dwelling place
for all mankind...
either Heaven or Hell.
And, whichever one chooses,
it is for eternity.
You will make millions of choices
as you move through life.
The place you choose for your spirit
to dwell forever
is the single most important choice
you will ever make.
Choose wisely with your soul.

© W. Mike Howell, 2017

(Reference: Holy Bible: John 14:2-3. The New King James Version.
1984 ed., Thomas Nelson Publishers).

UNHOLY FIRE

Fire...
One of the greatest
discoveries of humankind.
Used for good
or for evil.
Warmth in the cold,
Burning human flesh in war.
King Nebuchadnezzar used fire
to soften gold--
to shape it
into an image,
an image that
all people were
to fall down in front of
and worship.
Three brave, Jewish men refused,
knowing that their
God said, "There shall be no other
gods before me."
Shadrach, Meschack, and Abed-nego
did not fall down and worship the image.
Nebuchadnezzar was consumed
with rage and anger,
demanding his servants
to bring the disobedient trio to him,
and cast them into his
fiery, burning furnace of death,
designed especially for all who disobeyed him.
They bound the helpless men

in their coats, trousers, turbans
and other garments,
and cast them into the fiery furnace,
for an instantaneous,
but agonizingly horrible cremation.
The furnace flames were so hot
that they licked upward,
killing the servants who had thrown
the three good men into the burning pit.
Nebuchadnezzar, looking into the
blazing furnace, said,
"Did we not cast three men bound
into the midst of the fire?"
The servants answered, "True King."
The King said, "Look, I see four men loose,
walking in the midst of the fire;
and they are not
hurt,
and the form of the fourth is like the
Son of God."
When the King summoned the men
out of the fire,
only three men appeared.
Nebuchadnezzar spoke,
"Shadrach, Meshach, and Abed-nego,
servants of the most high God, come out,
and come here."
Their garments were not singed.
They had no smell of fire upon them.
Nebuchadnezzar said,
"Blessed be the God of Shadrach,

Meshach and Abed-nego,
Who sent His Angel and delivered
His servants who trusted Him... ."
The King continued,
"Therefore, I make a decree
that anyone
who speaks anything amiss
against their God
shall be cut in pieces
and their houses
shall be made an ash heap;
because there is no other God
who can deliver us like this."

(Reference: Holy Bible: Daniel 3:1-30.
New King James Version. 1984 ed., Thomas Nelson Publishers)

DANIEL'S BETRAYAL

Imagine the betrayal Daniel felt
when he,
being the King's favorite servant,
was thrown into a den
of hungry lions?
Why this fate,
after King Darius
had just appointed Daniel
as President over all his land?
It all had to do with
flaws in human character...
jealousy and competition
for public office,
hatred of an outsider's success.
This was a role that the locals
felt should
have been theirs.
Their own king's appointment
of
Daniel, a Babylonian outsider...
was just wrong,
a national injustice.
Daniel was also a Jew
who had been carried captive
to Babylon by Nebuchadnezzar,
a marauding king,
who had pillaged the Jews
by stealing the treasures
of Jerusalem,

along with four of its healthiest
and intellectually-gifted young boys.
Daniel, and the other boys,
were abducted from
that unholy land because they were
wise, educated, and healthy.
They were especially chosen
to serve in the King's Palace.
During their many years of service
to the King,
the four remained faithful to
the Holy God of the Jews.
Daniel became a loyal and favored
servant to that King
as well as to the later
King Darius.
Daniel's God-given abilities
allowed him to
correctly interpret
the King's visions and dreams.
None of the local Babylonian
wise men could adequately explain
King Darius' dreams.
Hatred-filled jealousy led these
Babylonians to set a trap
for Daniel
so that he might lose his
kingly favor and presidential position.
These angry men overwhelmingly
argued for the King to decree that
anyone making prayer to God

or any man,
be thrown into a den of hungry lions.
The King reluctantly made that decree.
The new law of the land
did not favor Daniel.
Daniel, being faithful to the true God,
flagrantly disobeyed this decree
by throwing open his windows
where he could be seen
kneeling and praying
three times a day.
The scheming, jealous Babylonians
spied on Daniel and caught him praying.
Daniel was caught in their devious trap.
They brought the news to King Darius,
The King was very upset.
He liked Daniel and did not want
his most knowledgeable servant thrown
Into the lion's den.
But he must not break his decree to his people.
The King spoke to Daniel,
"Thy God whom thou servest continually,
He will deliver thee."
Daniel was thrown in amongst the lions
and a stone sealed the mouth of the den.
The King did not sleep well that night.
He arose early and hurried to the den.
The King called out,
"Daniel, O Daniel, servant of the living God,
Whom thou servest continually,
He will deliver thee from the lions?"

Daniel answered,
"O King live forever.
My God hath sent his angel, and hath shut
the lions' mouth,
that they have not hurt me."
The king had Daniel taken out of the den,
and commanded that those angry men
who had accused him
to be cast into
the den of ravenously hungry lions.
But, that is not all:
the consequences of their
sins of jealousy would be
passed on immediately
to their children and wives,
who were also thrown to the hungry lions,
and likewise devoured.
The King then declared that in
every dominion of his kingdom
"men must tremble and fear
before the God of Daniel."

(Reference: Holy Bible: Daniel 6:1-26. New King James Version,
1984 ed., Thomas Nelson Publishers)

STAIRWAY TO HEAVEN

Imagine a man running from a would-be killer
through wildernesses and hot deserts.
Five hundred miles to get to safety.
And, this was only his first day.
It's not just any killer he is fleeing from,
It is his twin brother, Esau.
The fleeing man Jacob, by trickery,
and with the aid of his conniving mother,
has stolen Esau's birthright from
their father, Isaac.
Esau discovered what Jacob did
and he vowed to find and kill him!
And, now, Jacob is dead tired,
with a target on his back,
alone in the desert,
with wild beasts all around him.
He was beyond physical exhaustion.
He must rest.
Sleep must be had at any price.
He laid his head down
upon a stone.
It didn't matter that it was hard.
Sleep came fast,
along with this enigmatically strange dream.
"...and behold, a ladder was set up on the earth,
and its top reached to heaven;
and there the *angels* of God were
ascending and descending on it.
And behold, the Lord stood above it and said:

52

"I am the Lord God of Abraham your father
and the God of Isaac; the land on which you lie
I will give to you and your descendants."
"Also your descendants shall be as
dust of the earth;
you shall spread abroad to the west and the east,
to the north and the south;
and in your seed
all the families of the earth shall be blessed."
The key element in God's covenant
with Jacob is not so much the promised land,
but the fact that "all the families of the
earth shall be blessed" in Jacob
and his offspring.
This part of the covenant points
to the Messiah, Jesus Christ.
Then Jacob awoke from his sleep and said,
"Surely the Lord is in this place, and I
did not know it."
And he was afraid and said,
"How awesome is this place!
This is none other than the house of God,
and this is the gate of Heaven!"
Later, God told Jacob that his name
would no longer be "Jacob" but "Israel."
Jacob's twelve sons would make up the
future twelve tribes of Israel.
But, we digress from Jacob's strange dream.
It's possible significance deserves further analysis.
Jacob's dream--the ladder or stairway to Heaven--
should have great symbolism to Christians.

Three items were of great importance in the dream.
First, God strengthened his covenant to Jacob
that He had made to Abraham (Jacob's grandfather),
that the land of Palestine would eternally
belong to the people of Israel.
Second, the descending angels represent messengers
that God sends from Heaven down to His people on
Earth.
And, the ascending angels could represent man's
request and prayers upward to God in Heaven.
Finally, the most important part of the
dream is the ladder
which connects Heaven and Earth.
This is not a structural ladder,
but is Jesus Christ Himself.
He is the divine mediator
connecting Heaven to Earth.
And when His divine nature took on human form,
He was the connection between Earth to Heaven.
Jesus, while here on earth,
referred to Jacob's dream in
John 1:51 when he told Nathanael,
"...Most assuredly, I say to you,
hereafter ye shall see heaven open, and
the angels of God ascending and descending
upon the Son of Man."
Dreams were important
during Old Testament times,
And this one surely links
the Old Testament with
the New Testament Savior

as verified through
the words of Jesus Himself.

(References: Holy Bible: Text based on Genesis 27-32; John 1:51.
The New King James Version. 1984 ed., Thomas Nelson Publishers)

55

SATAN, THE GREAT TEMPTER

Water drops from the River Jordan
must have dripped from Jesus' hair
as John the Baptist
lifted His body from its cool waters.
And, tears must have fallen
from Jesus' eyes as he saw
Heaven open up.
"And the Holy Spirit descending in bodily form
like a dove upon Him,
and He heard a voice that came from heaven which
said,
'You are my beloved Son: in You I am
"well pleased '."
The message of John the Baptist had always been
"Repent, and
prepare the way of the Lord."
John had baptized many others besides Jesus,
and he had vehemently rebuked
against the evils of Herod,
so that
many considered that John could possibly
be the Christ himself.
But John answered, saying,
"I indeed baptize you
with water; but One mightier
than I is coming, whose sandal
strap I am not worthy to loose,
He will baptize you with the
Holy Spirit, and with fire... ."

And, after Jesus had been baptized,
He was filled with the Holy Spirit,
and was led by that Spirit into the wilderness.
One might think that the Son of God,
having received God's blessings
and
assurance that He, indeed,
was the Son of God,
would have been given a great feast,
a mansion with many servants,
and other special royalty treatments
befitting the long awaited Messiah.
But this was not to be so.
The spirit led Jesus into the
most inhospitable place
known in biblical times:
a terrifying desert, dry, hot,
and filled with dangerous animals,
thorny plants...and, worst of all,
Satan,
as a constant companion.
Jesus was to be put to the test by the
greatest tempter of evil that the
world has ever known,
Satan:
the leader of legions of
evil angels and demons.
God and the Archangel Michael
had long since kicked these evil ones
out of Heaven.
Unfortunately, they are all now

running rampant throughout our earthly realm,
wreaking havoc
and
destroying families and
individual souls by the millions.
This is the same Satan who had disguised
himself as the wise serpent in the
Garden of Eden,
and who brought evil
into our peaceful world.
Now, Jesus was in the God-forsaken desert
for forty days and nights,
alone with this vile King of Evil.
He could get no peace as
Satan tempted Him constantly...needling
Him to deny God.
Although Jesus was God in an earthly body,
He had earthly needs,
He was suffering from extreme human hunger.
He had not eaten for forty days and nights.
And the Devil taunted Him,
"If you are the Son of God,
command this stone to become bread."
But Jesus answered him,
"It is written, Man shall not live by
bread alone,
but by every word of God."
Then the Devil took Jesus
to a high mountain
so that all the Kingdoms of the world
could be seen at once.

Satan told Jesus, "If You will worship
before me,
all will be yours."
But Jesus said, "Get behind Me, Satan!
For it is written, 'You shall worship the
Lord your God,
and Him only you shall serve.' "
Then, Satan, the Great Tempter,
must have been filled with frustration...
His wily, evil schemes were not working
on the Son of God.
So, as a last resort, he took Jesus to Jerusalem,
and set Him on the highest point
of the temple.
He said, "If You are the Son of God,
throw Yourself
down from here.
"For it is written:
'He shall give His angels charge over you,
to keep you,'
"and, 'In their hands they shall bear you up,
lest you dash your foot against a stone.' "
Again, Jesus thwarted the Devil's temptation
by saying,
"It has been said, 'You shall not tempt
the Lord your God.' "
Satan, seeing his best temptations fail,
got a taste of what it is like
to tempt Jesus...who
was no ordinary man.
It is difficult to outmaneuver Satan,

But, it is impossible to outmaneuver Jesus.
The bewildered Devil then left Jesus.
But he laid in wait
for a more opportune time...
which is what devils and demons
do best.

© W. Mike Howell, 2017

(References: Holy Bible: Luke 4:1-13.
The New King James Version.
1984 ed., Thomas Nelson Publishers)

ONE ANGEL'S WRATH

Deserts in the Holy Land
can be scorching hot during the day
but freezing cold at night.
Deserts are often deadly quiet at night.
But quiet was not a description
of the desert that night
in early Hebrew history,
when one-hundred and eighty-five thousand
Philistines were sleeping
on the cold desert sands,
dreaming of their upcoming
total destruction of
the cities and nation of Israel.
(The warlike Philistines had lost their
independence to Assyria
and were fighting for that country),
Everything pointed to an upcoming bloodbath
of the people of Israel.
The sleeping soldiers must have filled
the quiet desert air with a
deafening chorus of thousands of snores,
coughs, and heavy breathings.
But these restful sounds changed
in a moment's time of deep sleep to
loud screams and cries of untold
horror, pain,
agony, and excruciating death
of the once sleeping soldiers.
Scripture states, "And it came to pass

on a certain night
that the angel of the Lord
went out,
and killed in the camp of the Assyrians
one hundred and eighty-five thousand;
and when people arose early in the morning,
there were the corpses--all dead."
God is our true Commander-in-Chief.
His soldiers are the angels of Heaven.
He commands thousands upon thousands
of them.
But, He does not need
massive armies of angels---
He only needs one.
Some scholars believe that
the term "angel of the Lord,"
is a reference to God Himself,
not just an angel.
God, alone, could certainly
have slain those sleeping Philistines.
But whether they were slain by an angel,
or by God, Himself,
this fact must be very disconcerting
to any army aiming to destroy
and pillage God's people.
Even today, those war-loving
and Israel-hating countries
surrounding tiny Israel
are hesitant to attack
God's chosen nation.
Most of them remember

biblical history,
and, in their mind's eye,
can vividly see
the memorable battle,
where nearly two-thousand
Assyrians (Philistines)
were unmercifully slaughtered
either by one of God's angels
or by God, Himself.

(References: Holy Bible: 2 Kings 19:35; 2 Chronicles 32:21.
The New King James Version, 1984 ed., Thomas Nelson Publishers)

THE ANGEL GABRIEL:
HIS MIRACLE BIRTH MISSIONS

God sends angels to earth
to carry out
His heavenly missions.
Some missions
seem more important
than others.
And some angels seem
to be more
favored than others.
Such an angel was Gabriel,
described as one
"who stands in the presence of God."
God had two missions
for Gabriel--that, when fulfilled--
would change humanity forever.
So Gabriel was sent to earth
to announce two miraculous
and impending
births:
first, that of John the Baptist,
and then, that of Jesus Christ.
These births were to be six
months apart.
Gabriel appeared first to Zacharias,
a very old, but righteous Temple priest.
Zacharias and wife Elizabeth
were a childless God-fearing couple,
who had prayed for years for a child.

Now they were both
decades beyond child bearing age.
For them to have a child
would be a miracle--
But, with God,
miracles are rather commonplace.
When Gabriel appeared
before Zacharias, he said,
"Do not be afraid, Zacharias,
for your prayer is heard;
and your wife Elizabeth
will bear you a son, and you shall call
his name John."
The baby John,
grew up to become John the Baptist,
who preached repentance to
prepare the people's hearts
to receive the Messiah,
Jesus Christ.
Six months after Gabriel revealed
the miracle birth of
John the Baptist,
he announced that an even more
miraculous birth would
soon occur:
the virgin birth of
Jesus Christ, the Messiah!
God then sent Gabriel
to a virgin named Mary.
She was betrothed to a young man
named Joseph.

And Gabriel, having come to Mary,
told her that she would conceive a Son,
not with Joseph,
but with the Holy Spirit.
Gabriel told her that
she should
name her baby" Jesus."
And, that her baby
would be the Son of God--
the Messiah promised by so many
Old Testament prophets!
What a miracle!
To modern-day non-Christians,
virgin birth
is considered to be
biologically impossible.
But, the world is full of doubters---
and so is Hell.
Luke 1:37 states,
"For with God nothing willbe impossible."
What an honor for Gabriel
to have been chosen to
announce perhaps
the two most important
births in history--
births that would change
human destiny forever.

(References: Holy Bible: Luke 1:1-80. The New King James Version,
Thomas Nelson Publishers).

LIGHT THAT TRANSFORMS
EVIL INTO GOOD

God's awesome powers permeate
the pages of Holy scripture.
Blinding light is often used
to make things happen.
Surely, no natural eyes
could have witnessed
the blinding brilliance of light
that radiated into the total darkness
at the creation.
God used blinding light to convert Saul,
a murderous persecutor of Christians.
Saul was on the road to Damascus
threatening to kill followers of Jesus.
Here is the Bible's vivid account:
"As he came near the city,
a bright light from heaven
suddenly flashed around him.
Saul fell to the ground
and heard a voice saying to him,
'Saul, Saul! Why are you
persecuting me?'
Saul said, 'Who are you,
Lord?'
The voice answered, 'I am Jesus, whom you
are persecuting,
Get up now and go into the city.
Someone there will tell you
what you must do.' "

A few verses later,
the Bible states,
"Soon he began to preach about Jesus
in the synagogues,
saying, 'Jesus is the Son of God.' "
God Light had instantly converted Saul into Paul
and evil into good.
Ordinary light from the sun
can transform chemical and physical reactions
throughout our solar system,
but is not the kind of light that converts
evil into good.
That unworldly light
is the transformative Light of God...
light that has the awesome power
to transform lost human souls
into earthly "beacons of light" for God.

© W. Mike Howell, 2017

(Reference: Holy Bible: Acts: 9:1-20. The New King James Version.
1984 ed., Thomas Nelson Publishers)

PRECIOUS MEMORIES,
UNSEEN ANGELS

As a young boy,
I have precious memories of
my mother singing religious songs.
Even now,
I can clearly hear
her kind voice
singing and humming
one of her favorite songs,
"Precious Memories."
This song still gives
me mixed emotions
of both comfort and sadness.
Comfort because of the words
of the song.
Sadness because my mother
is now gone,
and her words no longer echo
throughout the house.
But in my mind,
her words still linger
like a distant choir of holy angels.
I close my eyes
and hear my mother singing
these words,
"Precious memories, unseen angels,
sent from somewhere to my soul.
How they linger ever near me,
and the sacred past unfolds.

Precious memories how they linger,
How they ever flood my soul.
In the stillness of the midnight
precious sacred scenes unfold."

These moving lyrics
"...unseen angels sent from somewhere to my soul."
parallel many words from the Holy Bible.
Psalm 91:11 says,
"for he shall give his angels charge over thee,
to keep thee in all thy ways."
Unseen holy angels sent from above,
always point us toward God,
never away from Him.
And, in the process,
holy angels give comfort to our souls.
And, after all these years,
I still hear these, my mother's words,
echoing
throughout my mind,
"Precious memories, unseen angels,
sent from somewhere to my soul... ."

(References: Holy Bible: Psalm 91:11; Ephesians 3:18-19;
Hebrews 1:13. The New King James Version. 1984 ed.,
Thomas Nelson Publishers;
"Precious Memories" song lyrics by J.B.F Wright, 1925;
copyright Stamps-Baxter Co.).

THE GREATEST WORDS
EVER SPOKEN BY AN ANGEL

Search the Bible
through and through.
Try to find the most
beautiful and meaningful
words ever spoken by an Angel.
You will likely find them penned
in Matthew 28:1-7.
In these emotional passages,
the heartbroken
Mary Magdalene and the other Mary
came to see Jesus' tomb.
Upon arriving,
there was a great earthquake
because a thundering Angel of the Lord had
come down from Heaven and
rolled back the stone that
sealed the entrance
into Jesus' tomb.
The Angel then sat upon the stone.
This unnerving event
terrified the women
and the tomb guards shook for fear.
But the Angel said,
"Do not be afraid, for I know
that you seek Jesus
who was crucified.
He is not here; for He is risen,"
and he said, "Come see

the place where the Lord lay.
And go quickly and tell
His disciples that He is risen
from the dead... ."
Without these miraculous words
from the angel
there would be no forgiveness
of sins and salvation
for mankind.

(References: Holy Bible: Matthew 28:1-7.
The New King James Version. 1984 ed., Thomas Nelson Publishers:

LONELINESS

During times of spiritual
choices and crises,
you may feel all alone,
and your soul aches
to be set free.
Remember that you
are not really alone...
the good angels
and satanic demons
are always nearby...
wrestling with one another
to capture your every
subconscious and conscious thought.
Fighting for your soul
to join forces with them.
In these, your weakest moments,
make your greatest efforts
to choose sides with the good angels.
In doing so,
God, in His mercy,
and by grace,
will thwart the demons,
and
the incessant wrestling for your soul
will cease.
Your loneliness with vanish
as the morning fog
and your soul
will be set free.

Psalm 27:10 gives the lonely person
the assurance that
"When my father and mother forsake me,
then the Lord will take care of me."
During times of great loneliness,
we should hear, in our mind's ear,
echoes from
the old Christian hymn
"What a Friend We Have in Jesus"
The lyrics of this song remind us that
we are not alone,
and that the love of Jesus will help dispel
the loneliness that engulfs each of us
during times of spiritual choices
and crises.

© W. Mike Howell, 2017

(Reference: Holy Bible: Psalm 27:10.
The New King James Version. 1984 ed.,
Thomas Nelson Publishers;
lyrics to the hymn, "What a Friend We Have in Jesus",
by Joseph M. Scriven, 1855, The United Methodist
Hymnal Number 526)

WHERE DID ALL THE ANGELS GO?

It was near the end for Jesus,
and He knew it.
His teachings had been deemed
so radical and blasphemous
to the
chief priests and elders
that they sought
to bind Him
and deliver Him
to Caiaphas, the high priest.
There they would seek
false testimony against Jesus
to put Him to death.
When a group of them
armed with swords and clubs
approached Jesus,
and laid hands on Him
and took him,
a devout and angry
follower of Jesus
drew his sword
and cut off the ear
of the high priest.
One would think
that the follower
would be applauded
for fighting
to protect Jesus.
But, not so.

Jesus told him, "Put your sword in its place,
for all who take the sword will perish
by the sword.
Or do you think that I cannot now pray
to My Father,
and He will provide Me with more
than twelve legions of angels?"
But the angels did not appear
in a glorious cloud
to smite Jesus' enemies.
They were conspicuously
absent on that day.
And, therefore, Jesus was delivered
before Pontius Pilate, the governor,
who asked,
"What then shall I do with Jesus
who is called Christ?
They all said to him,
"Let Him be crucified!"
So, now where did all the angels go?
Jesus is headed for a sure death
on the cross,
but nowhere
can an angel be found.
The people placed a crown of thorns
on His head,
spat on Him,
mocked Him,
and struck Him on the head.
And, not a single angel appeared
to help Jesus in His most

humiliating moments.
The jeering people made Him bear
His own Cross.
They crucified Him.
Those who passed by him
on the cross
as He agonized with pain
and was slowly dying,
said to Him,
"You who destroy the temple
and build it in three days,
save Yourself!"
If you are the Son of God,
come down from the cross."
But Jesus,
growing weaker
with each heart beat
and loss of blood,
in unbearable pain,
said nothing.
No angels came to comfort Him.
Then, Jesus cried out,
saying "Eli, Eli, lama sabachthani?"
that is, "My God, My God,
why have you forsaken Me?"
So, where were all the angels?
And, where was God?
The Old Testament prophets
had spoken about this moment.
When Christ, the Messiah,
would take upon Himself

the sins of the world.
Jesus knew that
He was sent by His Father,
to die in this manner.
If the angels or God
had rescued Jesus.
He would not have been enabled
to die for our sins.
He knew that His
death on the cross
would wash away
the sins of the world.
He must be God's sacrificial lamb
for the salvation of mankind.
The angels and God
were likely
watching this whole significant
event unfold.
For the Christian,
Jesus' death meant
that belief in Him
and His teachings
would wash away
all of our sins.
So, we should be glad
that the angels and God
did not intervene, or stop,
that horrible death.
Without Jesus' death
there would not have been
His wondrous resurrection,

And victory over death.
So, all had gone
according to the plan,
a plan
that was an idea straight
from the mind of God,
and that was predicted
thousands of years before
by prophets of old.

(References: Holy Bible, New King James Version,
Thomas Nelson Publishers: Matthew 26:20-75; 27:1-66
and 28:1-6)

SODOM AND GOMORRAH

Evil winds blew across
the plains from the Dead Sea
toward the biblical cities of
Sodom and Gomorrah,
carrying
Satan and his evil angels,
who, like infectious diseases,
had
plagued the souls of the
people who lived there.
These demonic forces caused
the people to chose evil over good...
Satan over God.
God had seen enough of
the rampant sin and decaying souls
living in those vile cities.
God is patient, but His tolerance
is not without limits
especially
with unholy people who
continuously flaunt their depravity.
So He planned to destroy both cities,
obliterating all living things within them...
both sinful and righteous people.
Abraham pleaded with God
to spare the righteous ones.
God agreed to spare the cities only
if ten righteous people could be
found there.

But this was not possible.
However, there was one
righteous man, named Lot,
who was living in Sodom.
Two angels appeared to Lot
and told him that Sodom and Gomorrah
would be annihilated,
and that he should take his family,
flee the city, avoid the plains,
head for the safety of the mountains,
and do not look back.
It seems only human nature that when
someone tells you "not to look,"
an urge to look is almost overwhelming.
Lot's poor wife turned to take one last look,
at the awful fiery destruction, screams,
and burning flesh,
at a now scorched place once called Sodom.
There are consequences for not obeying God.
Lot's wife looked back,
and was immediately solidified
into a pillar of salt.
And the consequences of the evil in
Sodom and Gomorrah
was total annihilation.
Some have equated that horrible destruction
to that of an explosion from a nuclear bomb.
God's power must never be underestimated.
And, God's message is clear:
Worship God,
avoid all evil,

and your reward
will be the escape from
destruction,
and from the viral-like satanic diseases
that cause rot and decay of the eternal soul.

(References: Holy Bible: Genesis 18:20-33; 19:1-30.
The New King James Version. 1984 ed., Thomas Nelson Publishers)

SATAN'S FAVORITE TRICK

In this book of angel poems
it would be amiss to leave out
Satan,
as he, too,
was an angel,
albeit an evil one.
Satan, the king of all demons.
A beautiful angel,
named "Lucifer."
Even before the Archangel Michael
banished Satan
from Heaven
down to earth,
he was always fighting
against the one
true God.
He is a trickster.
The great deceiver.
The unequalled manipulator
of human behavior.
Satan's oldest trick
is to make something so desirable
that one gives into his deception.
And, then that person is hooked,
like the hopeless fish
that swallowed the bait
and is now struggling
with all of its might
to get free.

The fish did not see
the hook (or consequences) hidden inside
the bait.
Satan is much like a fisherman.
He presents a lure or bait to a human.
And, that lure has such a powerful attraction
that the human
grabs the bait,
is hooked,
and reeled into
Satan's control.
The human struggles to get free,
but the hook sinks deeper and deeper,
and the barb holds it there.
Satan first entered the stage of human life
when he approached Eve
in the Garden of Eden.
His earthly deception started there.
He disguised himself as a serpent
and tempted Eve
to eat the fruit
from the tree
in the midst of the garden.
Satan knew this tree
was the perfect bait for Eve.
It was the one tree
from which God had said,
"You shall not eat it,
nor shall you touch it,
lest you die."
Satan used this tree

and its irresistible fruit
as his greatest deceptive act
ever perpetrated ...
a lie that would change forever
the destiny of humanity...
by introducing sin into the world.
He made the fruit look so
alluring and delectable to eat.
Eve became overwhelmed
by her physical desires.
Furthermore, he told Eve
that she would not die
if she ate the fruit,
as God had forbidden her.
But, as a real bonus
when she ate it,
she would become like God,
knowing good and evil.
Unfortunately,
this temptation,
this deception,
hooked Eve and
she took the bait
and swallowed the hook.
She ate the tasty fruit
and gave some to her husband, Adam,
who also ate it.
The fruit didn't have true fish hooks
in it...
but, it had metaphorical hooks
of another nature.

They were immediately aware
that they were naked.
They hid themselves from the presence
of God.
To Eve,
God multiplied her sorrow and
He made child birth painful.
It was if a thousand hooks
were embedded in her womb.
He decreed that her husband
would rule over her.
But Adam did not escape,
He had Satan's hook in him also
at the moment
he took Eve's offering and ate it,
he became her accomplice.
For Adam's transgressions,
God cursed the ground
with thorns and thistles,
making farming difficult.
Adam was to labor and sweat
all the days of his life,
and eat bread until
he returned to the dust of the earth.
Throughout the Bible,
there are numerous verses
describing how Satan
uses our desires
to tempt us into sin.
He is the greatest liar
and can convince us

that if our desires
could all be fulfilled,
we would be happy
and not dependent upon God,
whose rules forbid us
to partake of certain
pleasurable sins in life.
And that has been the
goal of Satan
throughout human history.
For those who do not want
Satan's hooks in them,
they should flee from
all potentially sinful situations
as that is where Satan dwells.
Submission to Satan's temptations
always leads to misery
and lost souls,
and eternal separation
from God.
One can certainly avoid
this by abiding by the words
of James 4:7
which states,
"Therefore submit to God.
Resist the devil (Satan) and he will flee from you."

(Reference: Holy Bible: Genesis 3:1-19; James 4:7.
The New King James Version. 1984 ed., Thomas Nelson Publishers)

ANGELOLOGY

Angelology--the study of angels.
Supposedly scientific.
Subject to much debate.
Many scientifically-minded persons
find many reasons to disagree.
How can the scientific method
be used to
describe the nature of angels?
Can science gather empirical data
on spiritual subjects?
Angelologists have based their claims
on the Holy Bible,
and on human accounts of meeting angels.
According to them angels possess
at least eleven characteristics:
They are creatures of God.
They are bodiless spirits.
They have intelligence.
They carry God's messages.
They have a will.
They live in God's presence in heaven.
They obey God's will.
They can assume other bodily forms.
They influence our imagination.
They do not influence our free will.
They can move material things supernaturally.
Christians seem not to care much
about angelology.
After all,

faith is belief in things unseen--
God, Holy Spirit, and angels.
And, in things that can neither be
weighed nor measured.
But they believe in things that are surely
felt in the Christian's heart.
Our Savior,
Jesus Christ,
may be studied by historical facts,
He was seen and heard by thousands,
His words and actions were
carefully recorded by Biblical scholars
who were just as meticulous as
data-driven scientists.
He was as much an historical figure
as George Washington or Mother Teresa.
He died
on a cross
for our sins.
He was resurrected
with spiritual qualities.
Seen by hundreds.
Ascended to Heaven.
Belief in His words
is our only salvation.
He was not an angel,
but the Son of God.

Reference: Kreeft, Peter. 1995. *Angels (And Demons)*.
San Francisco: Ignatius. pages 28-29.

THE CREATION OF ANGELS:
A THEOLOGICAL CONTROVERY

Biblical mysteries abound.
Numerous spiritual questions exist.
Many have no answers.
But this does not stop
theologians.
Some expound
endlessly on biblical unknowns,
writing volumes of pure speculation
about the absolutely unknowable.
But intelligent persons who read their
works are not gullible.
Reason
quickly concludes,
that if the Bible does not state a fact
or describe an event,
it should remain unexplained.
One would do biblical truth
a grave injustice
by
inserting their own biased opinions
into Holy Scripture.
Theological conjecture
is highly suspect,
and should be avoided
by those who seek objective truths.
A classical example of
such a controversial event
is the unanswerable question,

"When did God create the angels?"
The Creation account in Genesis
tells us nothing about the creation of
angels.
Did God created them before the existence
of time and space?
Before the "Big Bang?"
Were they created during the Genesis Creation,
but their creation was simply not mentioned?
Though the Genesis creation account does
not tell us these things,
some say that angels had to be created
during the first six days because
Exodus 20:11 says,
"For in six days the Lord made the heavens
and the earth, the sea, and all that is in them,..."
This concept does not state when
the Lord made angels.
Job 38:4-7 tells about God
laying the foundations of the earth,
with all of its measurements,
and all of the sons of God (angels)
shouting for joy.
This would, for some theologians,
indicate that angels were created
early in the week of creation.
Other theologians take the easy way out of
the angel controversy
by saying, "One thing for sure is that angels
were created before the seventh day of creation."
This is because Genesis 2:1 says,

"Thus the heavens and the earth,
and all the host of them,
were finished."
Angels must have existed before
humans were created,
as the evil angel (Satan) appeared
in the Garden of Eden and,
disguised as a serpent, tempted Eve.
Apparently, at the end of the
great war in Heaven
between the evil angel, Lucifer (Satan),
and his forces,
against the good angel, Archangel Michael,
and his forces,
Lucifer was defeated and cast
down to earth
along with his evil angels (demons).
So, both evil and good angels must
have been created before man.
But we still do not know when.
Maybe during the first days of creation,
or during the expanse of timelessness
and spacelessness that existed
before the advent
of the biblical creation
when both time and space had their beginning.
Reason tells us that we do not know
when God created the angels.
This is not surprising
considering this is just one of hundreds
of biblical mysteries,

none of which take away from
the glory and power of God.
How the cosmos was created
is a mystery.
The transformation
of a heavenly God
into an earthly Jesus
is a mystery.
It is also a mystery
that He died for us,
but through His unexplainable resurrection
He lives.
It is a mystery that his shed blood
can wash away all of our earthly sins.
But, there is one "catch"
to His forgiveness of our sins--
we must believe in,
and worship the one true God.
The important events and facts
for man's salvation
are clearly laid out in biblical scriptures.
This is all we need to know.
Spending one's days intellectualizing
on exactly when God created the angels,
is a waste of one's precious time--
especially in light of our very short stay
here on planet earth.

(References: Holy Bible: Genesis 1:1-31; 2:1-3; Exodus 20:11;
Job 38:4-7.The New King James Version. 1984 ed., T. Nelson Publishers).

STREAMS

Like all streams
that flow to the sea,
all angels are
ideas that flow from the
mind of God.
Fast moving waters
at the stream's bend
undermine and collapse
the stream's banks
sending muddy mats
of dirt, trees, and tangled roots
churning downstream.
Thus, millennia after millennia,
floods, winds and droughts,
cause streams to change courses
and alter their sizes and shapes.

Angels, carrying out God's wishes,
are much like streams,
creeks, and rivers.
They can change shapes, sizes,
and morph into a variety of things.
Angels can appear as serpents
such as Satan (Genesis 3:1-19),
clouds (Acts 1:9-11)
or even humans (Hebrews 13:2).
Good angels have altered the
course of human history by:
battling Lucifer in Heaven,

slaying thousands of Philistines,
announcing the birth of John the Baptist,
announcing the birth of Jesus Christ,
and by performing scores of other missions.
Our minds are much like streams.
Will we choose the easy course of
flow taken by most of sinful humanity?
Or, will we flow down the most righteous,
but difficult
narrow passages of dangerous rapids
taken by the God-fearing few?
In doing so, we should not be afraid
because Psalms 91:11 says,
"For He shall give His angels
charge over you, to keep you
in all your ways."
Listen to the words of God.
Ponder them over and over in your mind.
Only God can alter the flow
of your life for the betterment
of yourself and all humankind.

© W. Mike Howell, 2016

(Reference: Holy Bible: Genesis 3:1-19;Acts 1:9-11;
Hebrews 13:2;Psalms 91:11. The New King James Version.
1984 ed., Thomas Nelson Publishers)

ANGELS: FANTASY OR REALITY?

Angel stories have been with us since the birth
of humankind.
They are sobering stories.
They are not to be equated with fantasy tales
such as Santa Claus, the Easter Bunny,
and the Tooth Fairy.
Angels are serious beings.
They were with Moses on Mount Horeb
at the burning bush.
They were present with Jesus at His birth,
at His baptism.
They comforted Jesus
in the wilderness,
after His forty days and nights
of temptations by Satan.
An angel strengthened Him
after His agony
in the Garden of Gethsemane.
They were there at His Resurrection.
Scores of such stories are interwoven
throughout the Bible,
involving innumerable people
from Genesis through Revelation...
stories of helping, protecting and communicating
with God's people.
These are not stories of childhood fantasies,
These are stories of adult reality.
Whether you believe angels exist or not,
is up to you.

God said that angels were His creations...
ethereal beings sent to protect those who
believe in Him.
Faithful people who believe in God,
would find it nearly impossible
not to believe in angels.

---Copyright, W. Mike Howell

(References: Holy Bible: Genesis 3:1-19; Acts 1:9-11;
Hebrews 13:2; Psalms 91:11. The New King James Version.
1984 ed., Thomas Nelson Publishers)

RECOMMENDED READINGS

Boa, Kenneth D., and Robert . M. Bowman Jr. 2007. *Sense and Nonsense ABOUT ANGELS & DEMONS.* Zondervan, Grand Rapids, MI.

Bonino, Serge-Thomas. 2016. *Angels and Demons: A Catholic Introduction.* The Catholic University of America Press, (English translation).

Chase, Steven. 2002. *Angelic Spirituality: Medieval Perspectives on the Ways of Angels.* (Translated by Steven Chase). Paulist Press, New York, NY/Mahwah, NJ.

Graham, Billy. 1986. *Angels, Angels, Angels, Angels*: *God's Secret Agents*, Grason, Minneapolis, MN.

Nowell, Irene. 2010. *101 Questions and Answers on Angels and Devils.* Paulist Press, New York, NY/Mahwah, NJ.

Williams, Peter. S. 2002. *The Case for Angels.* Paternoster Press, Carlisle, Cumbria, UK.

Wright, Vinita H. 2006. *A Catalogue of Angels: The Heavenly, the Fallen, and the Holy Ones Among Us.* Paraclete Press, Brewster, MA.

ABOUT THE AUTHOR

W. Mike Howell (Ph.D., University of Alabama)
is Professor of Biology *emeritus*, Samford University,
Birmingham, Alabama. He is the author of fifty peer-
reviewed scientific articles in biology, and five books.
He is a biological scientist, nature photographer, artist,
and poet.

He lives in Birmingham, AL with his wife, Mary, two
children, Todd and Kim, and three grand-children,
Holly, Conner, and Hunter.

* 9 7 8 0 6 9 2 9 5 9 2 3 7 *